Original title:
Blooming Silence

Copyright © 2024 Swan Charm
All rights reserved.

Author: Liisi Lendorav
ISBN HARDBACK: 978-9908-1-2161-1
ISBN PAPERBACK: 978-9908-1-2162-8
ISBN EBOOK: 978-9908-1-2163-5

Gentle Unfolding

Balloons rise high, colors ablaze,
Laughter dances through sunlit rays.
Friends gather close, hearts open wide,
In this moment, joy won't hide.

Tables adorned with sweet delights,
Candles flicker, casting warm lights.
Voices mingle like a soft tune,
Celebrating under the glow of the moon.

Silent Gardens

Whispers of petals in morning dew,
Sunshine kisses the blossoms anew.
A breeze carries fragrance with ease,
Nature's chorus, a symphony of peace.

Stepping stones lead through vibrant blooms,
Wandering hearts escape their glooms.
Every corner holds stories untold,
In this sacred space, warmth unfolds.

Meditative Mornings

Softly breaking dawn, a tender sight,
Birds sing sweet hymns, taking flight.
Tea steam rises, a comforting swirl,
In tranquil moments, our spirits unfurl.

Golden rays peek through the trees,
Awakening dreams on a gentle breeze.
Each heartbeat feels like a peaceful song,
In this stillness, we truly belong.

Void of Sound

Amidst the echoes of the night,
Stars twinkle softly, pure delight.
Moonlight bathes the world below,
In silence, vibrant energy flows.

Magic lingers in the subtle air,
A hush of wonder, everywhere.
When stillness reigns, hearts take flight,
In the void of sound, we find our light.

The Gentle Touch of Time

Time dances softly, a whisper in the breeze,
Moments like petals, floating with such ease.
Laughter spills freely, echoing in the air,
Joy weaves its magic, everywhere we share.

Candles flicker gently, casting shadows slight,
Memories awaken, in the shimmering light.
Hearts beat together, in a rhythmic embrace,
We celebrate life, in this sacred space.

Light's Tender Caress

Sunrise breaks softly, painting hues of gold,
A tapestry woven, with stories untold.
Children's laughter rings, a symphony of glee,
In this bright moment, we are truly free.

Festive balloons dance, swaying in delight,
The world feels alive, in this joyous sight.
Echoes of celebration, fill the vibrant day,
Hope's gentle whisper, guiding our way.

When Shadows Speak

Shadows softly linger, under the moon's grace,
Whispers of secrets, in the night's embrace.
Stars giggle brightly, in the velvet sky,
Each twinkle a promise, of dreams soaring high.

With every heartbeat, the night comes alive,
The magic of moments, together we thrive.
In this festive aura, love's warmth is near,
In shadows' soft rhythm, we conquer our fear.

Silent Reverie

In the hush of twilight, a silence profound,
Echoes of joy in the stillness abound.
Frosted air sparkles, under starlit dreams,
Life's gentle rhythm, flows like winding streams.

Whispers of wonder, linger in the night,
Hearts beating softly, in a shared delight.
Together we gather, in this moment's glow,
A silent reverie, where love overflows.

Beneath the Boughs

Joyful laughter fills the air,
Colors dance in the sunlight's glare.
Families gather, hand in hand,
Underneath the tree's grand stand.

Gifts wrapped in bright, cheerful hues,
Sweet aromas waft and amuse.
Tunes of merriment rise above,
Celebrating peace, laughter, and love.

Children play with gleaming eyes,
Chasing shadows under the skies.
Tales of wonder shared with glee,
Beneath the boughs, where hearts feel free.

As stars begin their evening show,
The warmth of togetherness will grow.
Hand in hand, we share this bliss,
In moments like this, we find our kiss.

Daydreams of Calm

Soft whispers in the breeze,
Floating dreams, we feel at ease.
Gentle waves lap at the shore,
Inviting peace we can't ignore.

Petals drift on summer air,
Nature's beauty everywhere.
Moments cherished, slow and clear,
In daydreams, worries disappear.

Sunset paints the sky in gold,
Stories of the day unfold.
With each breath, tranquility,
A heart at rest, so wild and free.

In this sanctuary of bliss,
We find our hearts, we find our kiss.
Daydreams linger, sweet and warm,
In stillness, we feel the charm.

The Essence of Solitude

In quiet corners, shadows lay,
Thoughts meander, drift away.
Amidst the silence, a spark ignites,
A gentle muse on peaceful nights.

Stars twinkle in the velvet dark,
Each one whispers a secret spark.
The heart finds solace in the still,
In solitude, it learns to feel.

Soft pages turn, a book in hand,
Every word a dream so grand.
Moments linger, like a sigh,
The essence of solitude, oh my.

Breaking dawn brings light anew,
But in solitude, I find my view.
In quietude, I find my song,
The serene whispers that make me strong.

Garden of Softness

A vibrant quilt of blooms appears,
In the garden, joy endears.
Colors splash, like laughter bright,
Filling hearts with pure delight.

Butterflies flit on gentle wings,
Nature's chorus sweetly sings.
Each petal soft, a tender touch,
In this garden, we love so much.

Sunshine filters through the trees,
Carrying the scent of ease.
In every corner, joy abounds,
In this haven, peace surrounds.

So let us wander hand in hand,
Through this meadow, lush and grand.
In the garden of softness, we play,
Woven together, come what may.

Subtle Awakening of the World

Soft whispers dance in the spring air,
Blossoms flutter, a sweet affair.
Colors awaken from winter's hold,
The world unfolds, vibrant and bold.

Sunlight spills through the branches wide,
Nature's canvas, a joyful ride.
Birds sing tunes of a fresh new day,
In the heart of spring, worries sway.

Stillness Wrapped in Color

Golden leaves twirl in the breeze,
Painting the ground with such ease.
Quiet moments, a festive cheer,
Embracing change, the end draws near.

Pumpkins glow in the fading light,
Harvest dreams take to flight.
Underneath the starry sky,
Whispers of joy drift softly by.

The Serenity Beneath the Surface

Waves shimmer under a gentle moon,
The world beneath hums a soft tune.
Colorful fish weave through the blue,
Harmony dances, a mystical view.

In the stillness, secrets reside,
Where serenity and joy collide.
Each ripple tells a tale to share,
Of life's blessings, tender and rare.

Embracing the Unvoiced

In the corners where shadows lie,
Laughter echoes without a sigh.
Hands clasped tight, spirits entwined,
Connecting souls, hearts aligned.

Festive lights twinkle, a guiding spark,
In silent moments, we leave our mark.
Through the unvoiced, we find our song,
In the festival of life, we all belong.

Laughter in the Distance

Joyful echoes fill the air,
Bright balloons are everywhere.
Families gather, hearts so light,
Dancing under stars so bright.

Children's laughter rings so clear,
Bringing warmth and festive cheer.
Colors twirl in brilliant sight,
Every moment feels just right.

Tables laden, food abounds,
Music plays, romance surrounds.
Fireworks crackle, burst, and glow,
In this night, our spirits flow.

Memories made in every smile,
Together we will stay awhile.
In this joy, we find our home,
Laughter calls, we are not alone.

Serenity Unfolding

In the garden, colors bloom,
Whispers dance in sweet perfume.
Butterflies flit, joy in flight,
Nature sings with pure delight.

Candles glow as shadows play,
Softly guiding end of day.
Fruits and sweets on tables shared,
Grateful hearts, all love declared.

Underneath the twinkling lights,
Voices mingle, hearts take flight.
Stories told of days gone by,
Laughter weaves, we touch the sky.

In this moment, peace enfolds,
Gathered near, a bond unfolds.
Serenity in every glance,
Together here, we find our chance.

Muffled Conversations

Laughter dances in the air,
Whispers float without a care.
Chatter mingles, hearts align,
Amid the glow of lights that shine.

Joyful tales exchanged in glee,
Sharing dreams like reverie.
Moments cherished, smiles wide,
In this warmth, our hearts abide.

Tunes of merriment surround,
Footsteps echo on the ground.
Festive spirits, brightened eyes,
In this night, true bliss lies.

With every hug and joyful cheer,
We find our loved ones gathered near.
Muffled voices, vibrant beats,
In celebration, life completes.

Where Echoes Sleep

Underneath the starlit skies,
Musical laughter softly flies.
Whispers dance like fireflies,
Where echoes rest, no goodbyes.

Colors twirl in brilliant flow,
Every heartbeat sets the glow.
Joy ignites the canvas bright,
Hopes and dreams take joyous flight.

Glimmers prance on silver streams,
Filling spaces with our dreams.
Echoes of love gently weep,
In this space, where echoes sleep.

The night weaves its tapestry,
Threads of joy, so wild and free.
Tales are told, and hearts entwine,
In this moment, all is fine.

Along the Dusk

As the sun begins to fade,
Colors burst, a joyful cascade.
Laughter spills like golden rays,
In the dusk, we share our plays.

Friends gather, stories unfold,
In this warmth, our hearts are bold.
Twinkling eyes and joyous sound,
In this magic, love is found.

Moments linger, sweet delight,
Dancing shadows paint the night.
Every smile a memory made,
Along the dusk, our fears are laid.

With the stars, our dreams ignite,
Chasing shadows, hearts take flight.
Together, we create a spark,
In the whispering of the dark.

Hushed Reflections

In silent corners, smiles reside,
Reflecting joy we cannot hide.
Mirth and laughter softly blend,
In hushed reflections, hearts transcend.

Candles flicker, lights aglow,
Treasures found in tales we know.
Promises made, with love's embrace,
In every moment, we find grace.

Time slows down in this retreat,
Every heartbeat, a rhythmic beat.
Whispers linger, warm and deep,
In the night, where dreams shall leap.

Gathered close, we share our fate,
With every glance, we celebrate.
Hushed reflections, voices clear,
In this moment, all is near.

Flourishing in Calm

Golden rays of sunshine play,
Children dance, it's a joyful day.
Colors bright in the gentle breeze,
Laughter rings among the trees.

Petals fall like cheerful dreams,
Nature's chorus flows in streams.
Hope and love are intertwined,
In this peace, our hearts aligned.

Warmth embraces every soul,
Moments cherished, we feel whole.
Hands entwined, we share our song,
In this calm, we all belong.

The Echo of Unheard Laughter

Whispers float on summer air,
Secrets shared without a care.
Joyous hearts in playful grace,
In this moment, we find our place.

Bright balloons against the sky,
Dreams are soaring, spirits fly.
Laughter dances through the crowd,
Echoes soft yet feeling loud.

Candles flicker in the night,
Hearts are warm, the mood is bright.
Stories told beneath the stars,
Magic hides in tiny sparrs.

Soft Echoes in Hidden Spaces

Among the trees where shadows play,
Secrets whisper, night meets day.
Fireflies twinkle, soft and clear,
In hidden spaces, love draws near.

Radiant blooms in twilight glow,
Songs of night begin to flow.
Soft refrains of joy resound,
In nature's arms, peace is found.

Waves of laughter chase the gloom,
In this haven, we find room.
Gentle breezes, stories flow,
In quiet corners, warmth will grow.

Nature's Gentle Secrets

Beneath the trees, the secrets lie,
Swaying leaves that touch the sky.
Golden hues of warmth and cheer,
Nature whispers, love is near.

Streams that giggle with delight,
Moonlit paths in soft twilight.
Every flower, every leaf,
Holds a promise, pure and brief.

With every gust, a dance unfolds,
Joyful stories yet untold.
In harmony, we all unite,
Nature's beauty, pure and bright.

Serenity's Embrace

In a garden where laughter flows,
Colors dance as the soft breeze blows,
Joyful hearts gather near and far,
Beneath the light of a twinkling star.

Bubbles rise into the blue,
Chasing dreams that feel so true,
Laughter echoes on the green,
In this moment, pure and serene.

Gifts wrapped in ribbons bright,
Shared stories weave through the night,
With every cheer and joyous toast,
We celebrate what we love most.

Nature's Soft Murmur

Birds sing sweetly as dawn awakes,
Petals open, benevolent flakes,
Sunshine kisses the morning dew,
A tapestry of vibrant hue.

The brook whispers a gentle rhyme,
Each note dances, transcending time,
Butterflies flutter in the air,
Nature's beauty beyond compare.

In the woods, we share a laugh,
Picnics laid on a sunlit path,
The world unites in joy and cheer,
In nature's warmth, we hold so dear.

Tranquil Resonance

Candles flicker with a gentle glow,
Magic swirls in the air, aglow,
Twirling dancers beneath the moon,
Hearts entwined in a sweet festoon.

The night hums with whispers soft,
As melodies lift our spirits aloft,
Shimmering lights twinkle and shine,
In this moment, we intertwine.

Each note a thread in the song we weave,
Binding dreams that we believe,
With every laugh and each embrace,
We find our joy in this sacred space.

Petals in the Air

Winds of spring carry scents so sweet,
With every blossom, our hearts compete,
In vibrant colors, life unfolds,
Nature's canvas, a sight to behold.

Laughter rises like blooms in spring,
An orchestra of joy we bring,
Underneath the sky so blue,
Friendship blossoms, pure and true.

Let the petals swirl and dance,
Each moment a fleeting chance,
To celebrate this festival bright,
And share our warmth in love's light.

Nature's Unvoiced Symphony

In fields where bright flowers sway,
The sun dances, lighting the day.
Birds sing sweetly, a joyous sound,
In this haven, peace is found.

Leaves rustle like whispers in air,
Nature's tune, a magic shared.
Laughter echoes through the trees,
Harmony swells with gentle breeze.

Over hills where shadows play,
The world glimmers in a vibrant way.
Each petal and leaf joins in song,
In this symphony, we belong.

Together we gather, hearts entwined,
In nature's arms, solace defined.
A festive spirit, wild and free,
In this moment, just you and me.

Where Serenity Blooms

Amidst fragrant gardens so bright,
The colors of joy ignite the night.
Every blossom wears a smile,
Inviting us to pause awhile.

Butterflies dance on gentle air,
In this wonder, we lose our care.
Soft petals brush against our skin,
In this realm, tranquility begins.

Candles flicker, casting a warm glow,
Lighting faces as laughter flows.
Under stars, dreams take flight,
In this sanctuary of pure delight.

Every heart beats in sweet time,
Creating a rhythm, a silent rhyme.
Together we find a sacred space,
Where serenity blooms, leaving its trace.

Soft Currents of Thought

Waves of laughter, softly glide,
Carrying dreams on the tide.
Each moment a ripple, a chance,
To step into life's joyous dance.

Clouds drift lazily, painting the sky,
While whispers of peace flit by.
Thoughts meander like streams at play,
In this essence, worries decay.

Glimmers of joy in every glance,
Creating a world where spirits prance.
In the warmth of the glowing sun,
The heart finds melody, joy begun.

Let currents of hope guide your way,
As festive colors weave the day.
In this flow, our souls unite,
Soft currents of thought bring delight.

Shadows in Bloom

In the twilight where shadows blend,
Whispers of laughter, a timeless friend.
The night blossoms with sparkling stars,
In this canvas, joy heals scars.

Candles flicker, casting a spell,
Each glow telling stories to tell.
Underneath a blanket of dreams,
Hearts unite in shimmering beams.

The moonlight dances, soft and free,
Inviting secrets, just you and me.
In this magic, fears intertwine,
As shadows in bloom, our spirits shine.

Together we weave the threads of night,
In each other, we find our light.
A festive spirit forever in tune,
With shadows in bloom beneath the moon.

Whispers of Stillness

Laughter spills in gentle streams,
Bright lights dance in moonlit dreams.
Joyful hearts in a woven throng,
Sing the sweetest, softest song.

Colors twirl in a vibrant haze,
Mirthful moments, the night ablaze.
Under stars, all worries cease,
In this world, we find our peace.

Candles flicker, shadows sway,
Every heartbeat leads the way.
Festivals of warmth and cheer,
Gather 'round, the joy is here.

Hand in hand, we share the glow,
In this fest, let love overflow.
Memories crafted, laughter shared,
In whispers of stillness, we are paired.

Petals in the Hush

Softly falling, petals drift,
Carried gently, spirits lift.
In the hush, the bells resound,
Magic whispers all around.

Breezes hum a sweet refrain,
Nature's beauty, like a chain.
Gathered joy in every eye,
Underneath the starry sky.

Voices mingle, hopes arise,
As warm laughter fills the skies.
Festive colors burst and play,
In this moment, here we stay.

With every smile, a spark ignites,
Petals dance in soft moonlight.
Celebration in sweet embrace,
In the hush, we find our grace.

Echoes of Quietude

In the stillness, laughter rings,
Echoes of joy, the heartstrings.
Candles glow with a tender might,
Whispers carry through the night.

Every shadow tells a tale,
In the quiet, spirits sail.
Hands entwined, a silent vow,
Together here, in this warm glow.

Time stands still, moments gleam,
Floating softly, like a dream.
In this peace, each soul unites,
Echoes bloom in starry nights.

Festive hearts beat loud and clear,
In the quiet, love draws near.
With every breath, we celebrate,
In echoes of quietude, we wait.

The Language of Serenity

In gentle winds, the stories flow,
Carried whispers, soft and slow.
Harmony in every sound,
Festive joy that knows no bound.

Branches sway in sweet embrace,
Every leaf a resting place.
Together, we weave our song,
In the language, we belong.

Stars above, our guiding lights,
Illuminating peaceful nights.
Fires crackle, laughter rings,
In serenity, our hearts take wing.

Gathered close, we celebrate,
In every moment, life's a fate.
With gentle hearts and open eyes,
In this language, love never dies.

Quiet Ripples

Beneath the trees, the laughter flows,
Children dance where the river goes.
Colors bright fill the air so sweet,
Joyful hearts in the summer heat.

Picnics spread on the greenest grass,
Time drifts gentle, as hours pass.
Songs of birds in the golden light,
Whispers of love, what a pure delight.

Glowing lanterns sway in the night,
Stars above twinkle, oh, what a sight!
Friendship blooms in the evening breeze,
Life's simple pleasures put minds at ease.

Memories made in this joyous throng,
Together we sing, we all belong.
With every cheer and every smile,
This festive spirit will linger awhile.

Beneath the Surface

Under the waves, a carnival bright,
Creatures dancing in shimmering light.
Secret worlds where the colors spill,
    Every moment, a thrill to fulfill.

With bubbles rising, the magic grows,
Happiness flows where the ocean glows.
Echoes of laughter, a playful embrace,
    Each splash of joy, a familiar face.

Coral gardens, vibrant and free,
Nature's wonders, a sight to see.
The rhythm of tides sings sweet harmony,
    Filling our souls with pure glee.

In the depths where the sun threads gold,
    Stories of old, yet to be told.
Beneath the surface, life swirls and twirls,
A festive dance of underwater pearls.

Gentle Caress of Daybreak

Morning whispers, a soft embrace,
Golden rays brush the sleepy face.
Nature awakens, the world alive,
In the hush of dawn, our spirits thrive.

Birds begin their sweet serenade,
Colors burst as the night does fade.
With each heartbeat, the day unfolds,
Stories of joy in warm sunlight told.

Sipping coffee, laughter shared,
Gentle moments, love declared.
In the quiet, hearts intertwine,
Together, we bask in the sunshine's shine.

As the hours dance, we sway and play,
In the gentle caress of the day.
With every heartbeat, every cheer,
We celebrate life, with those we hold dear.

In the Wake of Stillness

Evenings glow with a soft retreat,
Candles flicker, the shadows meet.
Warmth surrounds, as the twilight falls,
In each moment, the silence calls.

Crickets chirp in the gentle night,
Stars emerge, a breathtaking sight.
Whispers shared in the cooling breeze,
Stories linger amidst the trees.

Under the moon, we gather near,
Laughing softly, spreading cheer.
In the wake of stillness, we find our way,
Every heartbeat a tune that will play.

With promises made as the dusk descends,
Festive blossoms that friendship sends.
In these quiet moments, we find our bliss,
In the wake of stillness, a sweet, gentle kiss.

Whispers of the Wind

The breeze brings laughter, so light and free,
Dancing through branches, a joyful spree.
Colorful kites soar up in the sky,
As whispers of joy lift our spirits high.

Chimes of the flowers in radiant bloom,
Echoes of happiness banish all gloom.
Children are playing, their voices resound,
In this sweet moment, pure joy can be found.

Under the sun with its warm golden rays,
We gather together in festive displays.
Stories and laughter weave into the air,
Creating a tapestry, memories we share.

The whispers of wind, like a gentle embrace,
Fill hearts with gladness, bringing smiles to each face.
So let us rejoice in this day filled with cheer,
For the magic of life is truly here.

In the Absence of Sound

In the stillness, there's joy to be found,
Amidst the whispers, in the absence of sound.
Glowing lanterns twinkle in the night,
As the stars above shine ever so bright.

Festival colors paint the dark skies,
Filling the world with whispers and sighs.
Joy in our hearts as the night unfolds,
With stories of warmth and laughter retold.

Every smile glimmers like the moon's soft glow,
As friendships blossom, in the stillness, they grow.
In silent moments, we gather and stay,
Bound by the magic of the vibrant display.

Though sound may be absent, our spirits take flight,
In this peaceful haven, our hearts feel so light.
Together we revel beneath starlit expanse,
In the absence of sound, we lose ourselves in dance.

The Stillness Between

In the calm of twilight, the world holds its breath,
Moments of wonder, in silence, we rest.
A festival lantern, bright near the stream,
Glows softly, casting a warm, gentle beam.

Children gather round with their eyes open wide,
In the stillness between, where dreams coincide.
The world slows its pace, as magic takes hold,
In this quiet assembly, stories unfold.

Feasts are prepared with laughter and song,
In the stillness, we know where we belong.
Hands joining together, a united cheer,
Creating a symphony, sweet melodies near.

Let's celebrate moments, both simple and grand,
In the warmth of connection, we take a stand.
The stillness between, a time to reflect,
In the heart of our gathering, joy we collect.

Gardens of Glistening Dew

Morning breaks gently with soft golden light,
In gardens of dew, everything feels right.
Petals awaken, their colors so bright,
As laughter unfolds in the dawn's cheerful sight.

The fragrance of blooms fills the crisp, fresh air,
Inviting all hearts to dance without care.
Underneath skies painted blue and serene,
We cherish the beauty, youthful and keen.

Joy flows like rivers, unbound and so free,
In gardens of glistening dew, let us be.
Each moment a treasure, worth holding tight,
In this vibrant tapestry, we feel pure delight.

Celebrate life with a jubilant sound,
As nature surrounds us, our spirits are unbound.
In gardens of dew, we sow seeds of cheer,
For life is a festival when loved ones are near.

Quietude's Garden

In the garden where shadows dance,
Laughter twirls with every glance,
each blossom sings a vibrant tune,
underneath the bright full moon.

Butterflies paint the skies with grace,
warmth and joy in every space,
a picnic spread on emerald grass,
a day like this, we wish to last.

Friends together, hearts in bloom,
sharing stories, dispelling gloom,
a gentle breeze with whispers sweet,
quietude makes our joy complete.

As the sun begins to sink,
we gather, bond, and softly think,
beneath the stars, our spirits soar,
in Quietude's garden, we find more.

Unraveled Threads of Time

A tapestry of colors bright,
each thread a story, pure delight,
a festive air as laughter flows,
we weave our dreams as friendship grows.

Candles flicker, shadows sway,
underneath the twinkling array,
friends and memories intertwine,
creating moments so divine.

With every toast, our laughter rises,
like fireworks in happy sizes,
each story shared recalls the past,
in this tapestry, we're unsurpassed.

As night deepens, hearts align,
we dance and spin, our spirits shine,
through unravels, we find our way,
at this festival, forever stay.

Soft Echoes of Eternity

The stars above begin to gleam,
whispers float like wispy dreams,
in this night, with love so true,
every heartbeat speaks of you.

Laughter rings through open air,
gathered friends, a bond so rare,
sharing moments, sweet and bright,
in the soft echoes of the night.

Tales of joy and songs of cheer,
every word, a treasure dear,
time stands still, a gentle flow,
in this warmth, our spirits grow.

As dawn approaches, memories sway,
establish roots, we find our way,
in soft echoes, forever learn,
in festive hearts, our spirits burn.

The Peaceful Pause

In a world that rushes fast,
a moment's pause, a joy amassed,
a gathering where smiles align,
in the maps of hearts, we shine.

Bright banners wave, the music plays,
a gentle rhythm, a dance that sways,
underneath the sapphire sky,
celebrations lift us high.

With every cheer, the love expands,
a circle formed by hopeful hands,
united strong, we stand in grace,
hosannas sung in this bright space.

As twilight hugs the day goodnight,
we find our calm in pure delight,
this peaceful pause, our hearts embrace,
a festival of life, a sacred place.

The Language of Tranquility

In the sway of gentle breeze,
Laughter dances, minds at ease.
Colors bloom in warm embrace,
Joyful hearts in sacred space.

Underneath the starlit sky,
Whispers float, a sweet reply.
Harmony in every tone,
Together, never alone.

Candles flicker, shadows play,
Dreams alight, they find their way.
Echoes of a tender past,
Moments formed, forever cast.

Celebrate this tranquil night,
Wrapped in love, a pure delight.
Every heartbeat sings a song,
In this bliss, we all belong.

Hidden Harmonies

In the laughter of sweet friends,
Melodies that never end.
Silent thoughts begin to flow,
In the warmth, our spirits grow.

Underneath the moonlit glow,
Joyful secrets softly flow.
Every glance a knowing spark,
A symphony birthed from the dark.

Unseen threads that weave us tight,
Binding hearts in purest light.
We find magic in the still,
Every moment, every thrill.

Gather close, let shadows sway,
Whisper soft the words we say.
In this dance of heart and mind,
Hidden harmonies we find.

Soft Shadows

In twilight's gentle, soft embrace,
Silence wraps the cozy space.
Footsteps tread on dusky ground,
In the hush, sweet peace is found.

Stars ignite the evening's grace,
Softened whispers fill the place.
Moments freeze in air so light,
Shadows sway, taking flight.

Each twinkle holds a secret dream,
In the folds of night, we gleam.
A quiet cheer, a mindful pause,
Nature's rhythm, without cause.

Beneath the sky, our hopes unspool,
In soft shadows, we are whole.
Together we weave with delight,
Merging hearts in the night.

The Art of Hush

In the canvas of the night,
Silence wraps with sheer delight.
Every breath a cherished gift,
In stillness, spirits softly lift.

Moonlight paints the world anew,
Kisses soft, the heart breaks through.
Gentle glimmers, dreams take flight,
In the art of hush, all feels right.

Moments pause, as time slows down,
In this peace, we shed our frown.
Whispers speak of love's embrace,
In quietude, we find our place.

Celebrate the soft, sweet calm,
Every heartbeat sings a psalm.
Together here, we stay in tune,
Underneath the watchful moon.

The Still Dance of Leaves

In the breeze, the leaves do sway,
Twinkling like stars on a bright day.
Their whispers call, a joyful tune,
As autumn glows beneath the moon.

Golden hues in bright sunlight,
Nature's stage, such pure delight.
With every rustle, hearts align,
In stillness, spirits intertwine.

Amidst the trees, laughter rings,
A celebration of simple things.
Each leaf a story, each twirl a dream,
Together we dance, a vibrant theme.

As twilight falls and shadows weave,
We find our joy in the still dance of leaves.
Nature's symphony, soft and sweet,
In this moment, our hearts skip a beat.

Solitude's Serenade

In shadows deep, a melody flows,
Whispers of peace where silence grows.
A gentle calm, wrapped in a sigh,
As stars awaken in the night sky.

The moonlight paints with silver hue,
Each note a dream, each breath anew.
In solitude, our hearts explore,
The magic hidden at the core.

With every strum of the soft guitar,
Songs of the soul, our guiding star.
Fingers dance lightly on the strings,
Creating joy that solitude brings.

In quiet moments, the world stands still,
A serenade of the heart's own will.
In this soft glow, we find our way,
Through solitude's song, we choose to stay.

Echoes of the Unspoken

In every glance, a secret shared,
In silence deep, our souls laid bare.
Whispers linger, tangled and sweet,
Echoes of thoughts, where hearts compete.

With every pause, a story unfolds,
In the warmth of moments, love beholds.
In unvoiced dreams, we find our path,
In shared breaths, we hold the aftermath.

Through gentle smiles, our language flows,
In shadows cast, the bond just grows.
In unspoken words, a deeper dance,
A melody ripe, awaiting chance.

The night wraps close as stars ignite,
In unsaid echoes, we take flight.
Embraced in the silence, we find a tune,
In echoes of love, we are immune.

Silent Resonance

In stillness found, a pulse reveals,
A quiet thrum, a heart that feels.
Each breath a promise, softly cast,
In silent resonance, shadows past.

Beneath the stars, we pause and dream,
In whispered night, a gentle stream.
The world around fades in the hush,
Creating space for hearts to rush.

With every twinkling, joy unfolds,
The night wrapped deep in tales retold.
In silence shared, our souls ignite,
As we dance in sync 'neath the silver light.

In quiet moments, love finds grace,
In silent harmony, we embrace.
Together we tread on softest ground,
Where silent resonance can be found.

Dreams in the Quiet

In the stillness, laughter rings,
Whispers soft, like gentle wings.
Stars above, a twinkling show,
Beneath the moon's warm, silver glow.

Children's joy, a playful tune,
Lovers dance beneath the moon.
Magic floats upon the air,
In this moment, nothing compares.

Softly twinkling lights align,
Every heartbeat feels divine.
Dreams take flight on wings of night,
In quietude, the world feels right.

Love encircles all we see,
In this dream, forever free.
With every breath, our spirits soar,
In dreams of quiet, we explore.

Quietude's Canvas

Brushstrokes of a gentle breeze,
Canvas painted with the trees.
Sunlight dapples through the leaves,
Nature's beauty, all it weaves.

Colors splash in joyful cheer,
Nature sings, inviting near.
Every petal, every hue,
Whispers secrets old and true.

Gathered friends with laughter bright,
Filling hearts with pure delight.
Moments shared under the sky,
In quietude, our spirits fly.

The melody of peace we find,
As stars gather, intertwined.
Night descends, our souls take flight,
In the canvas of the night.

Secrets of the Meadow

In the meadow, wild and free,
Nature hides a mystery.
Petals dance on morning dew,
Whispers soft, both warm and true.

Crickets sing their evening song,
A symphony where hearts belong.
Rustling leaves in soft embrace,
In this haven, we find grace.

Breezes weave through blades of green,
Secrets in each corner seen.
Dancing fireflies light the way,
Guiding dreams 'til break of day.

With every step, a rhythm plays,
In the meadow's warm displays.
Wild and gentle, joy we heed,
In whispers, nature's heart does lead.

The Poetry of Peace

In stillness, echoes softly sound,
Where the heartache cannot surround.
Calm streams flow, a tranquil hymn,
Beneath the sky, so vast and dim.

Golden rays of sunbeam shine,
Whispers of a love divine.
Hearts unite beneath the trees,
Finding solace in the breeze.

Every moment, a soothing grace,
In nature's arms, we find our place.
Gentle laughter fills the air,
In peace, we breathe without a care.

Near the water's serene embrace,
Life unfolds at a gentle pace.
With every sigh, our spirits dance,
In the poetry of peace, we advance.

The Art of Soft Shadows

In gardens bright, the laughter flows,
Glimmers dance where sunlight glows.
Colors swirl in joyous play,
As breezes hum, inviting sway.

Banners wave in hues so bold,
Stories of joy in whispers told.
The sun dips low, a golden thread,
Where dreams weave softly, gently spread.

Children chase the fleeting light,
With every heartbeat, pure delight.
The world adorned in festive cheer,
Celebrations far and near.

As twilight paints the sky in pink,
We gather round, the glasses clink.
In every gaze, the magic flows,
In the art of soft shadows, love grows.

Silent Petals Unfurling

In gentle gardens where silence reigns,
Petals whisper secrets, love's refrains.
Each bloom unfolds with tender grace,
A dance of colors in nature's embrace.

Beneath the shade of ancient trees,
Joyful songs drift with the breeze.
The sun peeks through in golden rays,
Igniting smiles in soft arrays.

Laughter echoes, hearts unite,
In the stillness, pure delight.
The fragrant air of hopes anew,
Each moment cherished, bright and true.

As night descends with twinkling stars,
We celebrate, forgetting scars.
With silent petals, love is swirling,
In every heart, the joy is unfurling.

Dreams in the Quiet Grove

In the quiet grove where shadows play,
Whispers carry hopes away.
Moonlight drapes the earth in gold,
A tapestry of dreams unfolds.

Beneath the arches where soft winds sigh,
Children laugh and spirits fly.
Fireflies blink in tender glee,
Guardians of this reverie.

With every rustle, secrets known,
In nature's heart, we feel at home.
Buds awaken, colors blend,
In dreams, we find our hearts extend.

As the stars shimmer high above,
We gather close, wrapped in love.
In the quiet grove, we often roam,
Crafting memories, building home.

Mute Conversations of Spring

In gardens where the blossoms sway,
Mute conversations softly play.
Petals drift in sweet embrace,
Painting joy upon each face.

The brook dances, a merry tune,
While light spills down, a silver moon.
Birds serenade with cheerful calls,
As each moment blissfully falls.

Underneath the canopy wide,
Laughter flows like a gentle tide.
Every glance a shared delight,
In the spring's warmth, hearts take flight.

As twilight whispers, the day must part,
In silent bonds, we share our heart.
With mute conversations, love will spring,
Rooted deep in everything.

Unspoken Gardens

In gardens lush, the colors play,
A symphony of blooms displays.
Whispers of joy in every petal,
A dance of life, love's sweet medal.

Laughter echoes through the trees,
Carried forth on gentle breeze.
Bright lanterns twinkle in delight,
Casting warmth in the cool night.

Joyful hearts gather around,
In this haven, peace is found.
The fragrance rich in every hue,
Tells of stories old and new.

In unspoken gardens we stand,
Embracing dreams hand in hand.
Together in this vibrant space,
Where time slows down, a sweet embrace.

Veils of Tranquility

Beneath the stars, the shadows sway,
In softest silk, the night holds sway.
Velvet whispers serenade the air,
Wrapped in peace, beyond compare.

Moonlit pathways gently gleam,
Casting forth a wistful dream.
As laughter beckons, spirits rise,
In a tranquil dance 'neath endless skies.

The world a canvas brushed with light,
Each moment fleeting, pure delight.
With every breath, our hearts align,
In veils of calm, our souls entwine.

Here joy resides, so deeply found,
In tender silences, love unbound.
A celebration soft and bright,
In veils of tranquility, pure light.

Secrets in the Stillness

Secrets whisper in the air,
In every silence, tales laid bare.
Nature's pulse beats soft and slow,
In the stillness, joy will flow.

Golden sunbeams gently play,
On fields where wishes drift away.
Each petal, like a sigh of grace,
Holds the magic of this place.

In quiet corners, dreams unfold,
Stories shared, both new and old.
A tranquil refuge we create,
In secret moments, we await.

With every heartbeat, laughter sings,
A festive joy that nature brings.
In shadows long, hope will blaze,
In secrets found, we find our ways.

When Time Lingers Softly

When time lingers, moments gleam,
In the twilight, hearts redeem.
Every laugh, a twinkling star,
As memories bloom, near and far.

The world awakens, vibrant and bright,
In the embrace of sweet moonlight.
Children dance, their spirits free,
In this enchanting reverie.

Softly spoken words of cheer,
Echo through the atmosphere.
Holding close what we adore,
As fragrance sweetens, we explore.

In gatherings where love is found,
Every heartbeat, a joyful sound.
When time lingers, life enchants,
In those moments, joy still prances.

The Grace of Quiet Moments

In the soft glow of fading light,
Laughter dances, spirits take flight.
Candles flicker, shadows sway,
Joyful whispers mark the day.

Hearts entwined in simple cheer,
Sharing secrets, holding dear.
Every glance, a story shared,
In quiet grace, we feel prepared.

A tapestry of smiles and love,
Underneath the stars above.
Time pauses in this sweet embrace,
A fleeting moment, a sacred space.

As night unfolds its velvet hue,
We cherish all these bonds so true.
With every laugh, we celebrate,
The grace of moments we create.

Whispering Blooms

In gardens where the soft winds blow,
Colors clash in vibrant show.
Petals dance in morning dew,
Nature's canvas comes alive anew.

Delicate scents fill the air,
Laughing friends, without a care.
Sunshine spills on leafy streams,
In playful waves of golden beams.

Butterflies flirt, a gentle play,
Frolicking in the light of day.
Together here, we find our bliss,
Among the blooms, a sweetened kiss.

Moments stitch our hearts in time,
In whispered blooms, such joy we find.
With every petal, hopes arise,
In nature's arms, the world feels wise.

Murmurs of the Heart

Underneath the twinkling stars,
We gather close, forgetting scars.
Softly spoken, dreams take flight,
Murmurs echo in the night.

Each heartbeat tells a story rare,
In gentle words, we boldly share.
Laughter peals like chimes in air,
A melody of love and care.

With every hug and warming grin,
We stoke the fires of what's within.
In this cocoon, we feel so free,
Murmurs weave our tapestry.

Life's sweet rhythm sways us near,
In echoes soft, we shed our fear.
Through murmurings, our spirits soar,
In heart's embrace forevermore.

Huddled in Harmony

In the glow of the evening's grace,
Together, we find our place.
Warmth ignites with every song,
Huddled close, where we belong.

Voices blend in soft refrain,
Carrying joy like gentle rain.
Candles flicker, shadows blend,
Moments cherished, hearts transcend.

With laughter's spark, the room ignites,
In dance and glee, we reach new heights.
Stories shared, our souls align,
In harmony, we brightly shine.

The night embraces, whispers sweet,
With every embrace, our spirits meet.
In this circle, love is found,
Huddled close, in joy, we're bound.

Hushed Voices of the Earth

In twilight's glow, we gather near,
Laughter dances, joy sincere.
Golden lights twinkle in the night,
Hearts echo warmth, spirits take flight.

Beneath the stars, we share a jest,
In friendship's bond, we find our rest.
Waves of cheer in the evening air,
The world is still, and we all share.

With music soft, a gentle tune,
We sway along 'neath the silver moon.
Nature's whispers wrap us tight,
In this moment, all feels right.

A tapestry of dreams we weave,
In harmony, we laugh and believe.
The night is young, no need to part,
Hushed voices bloom from every heart.

Traces of Silent Growth

Amidst the petals, colors bright,
Nature whispers in pure delight.
Buds unfurl with silent grace,
Creating beauty in every space.

The air is sweet with fragrant bloom,
Joy emerges from winter's gloom.
Each gentle touch, a story told,
In every sprout, there lies pure gold.

Sunbeams dance on leaves so green,
Nature's canvas, endlessly seen.
Life unfolds like a songbird's tune,
In harmony, we find our boon.

Together we celebrate this phase,
As laughter echoes through sunlit ways.
Embrace the joy of this vibrant earth,
For in each moment, there's endless worth.

The Pause Before Dawn

As darkness fades, a hush ensues,
The world awaits the morning hues.
Stars begin their soft goodbye,
With whispers of dreams that pass by.

A gentle glow spills from the sky,
Colors merge as night says shy.
The air is thick with silent cheer,
In this moment, all feels clear.

Birds prepare their joyful calls,
Nature listens as night withdraws.
Hearts align with the coming light,
We breathe in hope, embracing the bright.

With each flicker, a spark ignites,
The pause awakens all delights.
Together we stand, hand in hand,
Awaiting dawn across the land.

Murmurs Among the Leaves

In wooded realms where shadows lay,
Murmurs of life start to sway.
Leaves embark on a gentle dance,
Caressed by breezes, a sweet romance.

Sunlight filters through branches wide,
Nature's secrets, soft and tried.
Squirrels leap with joyful grace,
In playful tunes, they find their place.

Whispers rise like a tender sigh,
Life's melody beneath the sky.
The forest holds its festive cheer,
Each rustle speaks, for all to hear.

Together we celebrate this scene,
In earthly wonders, pure and serene.
With every murmur, hearts align,
In unity, we truly shine.

In the Embrace of Quietude

In the glow of twilight's hue,
Laughter dances on the breeze,
Stars begin to peek anew,
Whispers carried through the trees.

Candles flicker, soft and bright,
Joyous hearts in harmony,
Moments wrapped in pure delight,
Together, we are wild and free.

Echoes of a song so sweet,
Footsteps light on summer grass,
Memories in laughter meet,
Time, it shimmers as we pass.

Underneath the moonlit sky,
Every soul feels close and warm,
With a spark, we rise up high,
In the stillness, we transform.

Whispers of Dawn

As the sun begins to rise,
Colors brush the waking morn,
Nature sings with softest sighs,
In this light, the day is born.

Fields of gold and skies of blue,
Laughter mingles with the dew,
Hope and joy in every hue,
All our dreams feel bright and true.

Gathered friends with hearts so light,
Share our stories, laugh and play,
In the warmth of morning's sight,
We embrace the brand new day.

Whispers echo softly clear,
As we dance to rhythms sweet,
Every moment drawing near,
Life, a joyous, endless beat.

Gentle Quietude

In the garden, soft and rare,
Petals fall like whispered prayers,
In the air, a gentle care,
Beauty blooms beyond compares.

With each smile, the world awakes,
In the silence, love abounds,
Every laugh a joy that breaks,
Harmony in all the sounds.

Mellow tones of twilight's call,
Dancing shadows, soft and fair,
Together, we shall rise and fall,
In this moment, evergreen air.

Caught in frames of lilting light,
Time stands still, as hearts align,
In the hush, everything's right,
Festive spirits intertwine.

Echoes in Stillness

In the night, where dreams take flight,
Stars align in silver lines,
Music wrapped in pure delight,
Where the universe defines.

Candles glow with vibrant cheer,
Softly glowing, hearts entwine,
Every heartbeat drawing near,
In this magic, all is fine.

Ghostly echoes of our past,
Fill the air with sweetened cheer,
In this moment, love is cast,
With each smile, we draw near.

Gentle breezes, whispers sweet,
Carry laughter in their wake,
Every moment feels complete,
In the magic that we make.

Whims of the Wind

The breeze dances free, a playful delight,
Whispers of joy as day turns to night.
Kites soar above in a colorful array,
Under the sun, we laugh and we play.

Leaves flutter softly, a rustling cheer,
Each gust of the wind brings loved ones near.
From branches they sway, a sweet serenade,
Nature's own party, in the sunbeams laid.

Joyous hearts merge with the rhythm so grand,
With smiles that bloom like flowers in hand.
Lifting us higher, the wonders unfurl,
In this fest of life, we spin and we twirl.

Come dance with the wind, let your spirit ignite,
Embrace the adventure, let everything light.
In the whims of the wind, we find all we need,
Together, forever, we dream and we breathe.

Still Waters Run Deep

By the edge of the lake, the reflections invite,
Silvery ripples that shimmer and delight.
Picnics abound with laughter and cheer,
As ducks glide gracefully, drawing us near.

In the shade of the trees, shadows play tricks,
Children chase dreams, with their twirling sticks.
The sun filters through, a beautiful hue,
Creating a canvas, both peaceful and new.

Songs fill the air, a sweet melody,
Echoes of joy, where hearts feel so free.
A moment suspended, time slows its race,
With each gentle breeze, life finds its place.

Still waters embrace all the love that we share,
In this tranquil spot, we answer the prayer.
A gathering of souls, both near and divine,
In the harmony found, our spirits align.

In the Heart of Calm

Where the wildflowers bloom, in colors so bright,
The world takes a pause, everything feels right.
With gentle embraces from sun's warm glow,
In the heart of calm, all our worries can go.

Birds sing sweet songs in the forgiving air,
Their melodies weave through the moments we share.
Each laughter and smile, a treasure held dear,
In this peaceful haven, it's love we revere.

The butterflies twirl in a whimsical dance,
Nature invites us to take a chance.
With every soft breeze, joy comes into play,
In the heart of calm, we forever will stay.

As stars sparkle bright in the twilight's embrace,
Our hearts swell with warmth in this magical place.
Together in silence, our spirits align,
In the heart of calm, we eternally shine.

A Symphony of Silence

In twilight's soft glow, the world fades away,
A symphony whispers, in twilight we sway.
The stars twinkle softly, like notes in the night,
Creating a balance of shadow and light.

The hush of the evening enfolds us with care,
Each heartbeat resounding, a beautiful flare.
We gather as one, in dreams we confide,
In the symphony born from the stillness inside.

As fireflies flicker, like rhythms in flight,
Their dance brings us closer, twinkling so bright.
The magic of moments dances in trance,
A symphony played in soft silken glance.

In silence we revel, in peace we exist,
This harmony blessed, a soft, gentle mist.
Embracing the quiet, our hearts intertwine,
In a symphony of silence, so pure and divine.

Where Silence Takes Root

In a grove where laughter hides,
Whispers dance upon the breeze,
Colors burst as joy collides,
Nature hums as daylight frees.

Underneath the spreading trees,
Children play with carefree glee,
Every shadow seems to tease,
Invisible hearts sing with glee.

Joyful echoes fill the air,
Every moment crafted bright,
In this space, no room for care,
Only peace and pure delight.

As the sun begins to fade,
Colors paint the sky in gold,
In this sweet, enchanting glade,
Festive stories all unfold.

The Gentle Breath of Dawn

When the sky begins to blush,
Softest hues of pink arise,
Nature stirs, a tender rush,
In the hush, the world complies.

Birds awaken in delight,
Notes of joy begin to soar,
With the warmth of morning light,
Every heart feels rich and more.

Flowers bloom, their petals wide,
Dewy jewels catch the sun,
In the warmth, we all abide,
Celebrating life as one.

As dawn folds into the day,
Songs of children fill the air,
In this festive, vibrant play,
Every heart is free to share.

A Symphony of Softness

Swaying trees in gentle play,
Leaves dance softly to the ground,
Nature's song demands we stay,
In this beauty, peace is found.

Every whisper, calm and sweet,
Brings a smile, ignites the soul,
In the rhythm, hearts will meet,
Together, they will feel whole.

As the brook begins to sing,
Notes of laughter fill the space,
In this perfect, tender spring,
Joy and love intertwine with grace.

Underneath the azure skies,
Festive moments come alive,
In each glance, a spark resides,
In this symphony, we thrive.

Quiet Reflections of Nature

In a garden, softly glows,
Flowers whisper tales untold,
In their stillness, silence flows,
Every petal shines like gold.

Rippling waters, clear and pure,
Mirror skies of azure blue,
In their depths, we find a cure,
Nature's magic, ever true.

Clouds drift lazily above,
Painting dreams across the day,
In this realm of soothing love,
Festival of life on display.

As the sun begins to dip,
Shadows stretch across the land,
Hearts unite in gentle trip,
In this quiet, hand in hand.

Unseen Symphony

Notes of joy dance around,
In the air, laughter is found.
Colors burst in the sky,
As hearts swell, spirits fly.

Bubbles float with delight,
Candles flicker in the night.
Together we sing and cheer,
Every moment, precious and near.

Joyful voices blend and sway,
In this night, we wish to stay.
With each step, a beat anew,
The unseen symphony shines through.

Let's raise a toast, a cheer,
To moments cherished, held dear.
In this festive, vibrant glow,
Together, let our spirits flow.

Beneath the Quiet Canopy

Beneath the trees, shadows play,
Golden leaves drift and sway.
Whispers of the breeze sing low,
Nature's rhythm, a soft glow.

Lanterns twinkle in the dark,
Creating magic, a lively spark.
Soft laughter fills the gentle night,
As friends gather, hearts feel light.

Songs of joy echo through,
In this haven, all feels new.
Each story shared, a precious thread,
Woven tightly, laughter spread.

Amidst the stars, we find our bliss,
Every hug, each heartfelt kiss.
Beneath the quiet, joyous sighs,
The canopy holds our sweetest ties.

Echoing Thoughts

Echoes of laughter ring clear,
In the air, there is cheer.
Bright fireworks light the sky,
As dreams reach, soaring high.

Hands held in friendship's embrace,
Each smile paints a warm grace.
Together we weave joyful tales,
Setting out on vibrant trails.

Time may flow, yet stays still,
As hearts beat with a joyful thrill.
In shared moments, we find our song,
Together is where we all belong.

A chorus of vibrant delight,
Guiding us through the night.
With every thought, a dance unfolds,
In this festive spirit, life holds.

Petal's Breath

Petals drift on a warm breeze,
Whispers of spring stir the trees.
Bright blooms, a colorful array,
In their presence, worries sway.

Festive drinks raise up high,
Smiling faces fill the sky.
Every toast, a memory made,
In this lively, joyous parade.

Children laugh, joyfully run,
Chasing shadows under the sun.
Together we gather, hearts aglow,
In the garden where good vibes flow.

As night falls, stars begin to twinkle,
With every pulse, our spirits crinkle.
Beneath the moon's gentle caress,
We celebrate, feeling truly blessed.

www.ingramcontent.com/pod-product-compliance
Ingram Content Group UK Ltd.
Pitfield, Milton Keynes, MK11 3LW, UK
UKHW030844221224
452712UK00006B/544